SUMMERLIN

W9-ANP-820

BRICKS

Graham Rickard

Thomson Learning
New York

Books in this series

Bricks

Electricity

Gas

Glass

Oil

Paper

Plastics

Steel

Water

Wood

Cover: (Main picture) A bricklayer building a wall. (Top right) A very old mausoleum built of baked brick in Central Asia.

First published in the
United States in 1993 by
Thomson Learning
115 Fifth Avenue
New York, NY 10003

First published in 1991 by
Wayland (Publishers) Ltd

Cataloging-in-Publication Data applied for

ISBN 1-56847-046-0

Printed in Italy

Contents

All the words that appear in **bold** are explained in the glossary on page 30.

What are bricks?

Bricks are small building blocks of clay or mud. They have been dried in the sun or baked in a **kiln** to make them hard and strong. Builders use bricks to make walls. To build a wall, builders lay bricks in lines, one on top of another, and stick them together with clay or **mortar**.

The size of bricks varies from one country to another, but most modern bricks are small enough to hold in one hand. Bricks are usually twice as long as they are wide—a standard brick measures $3\frac{5}{8}$ x $2\frac{1}{4}$ x $7\frac{5}{8}$ inches.

Above *Bricks are commonly used to build modern cities such as New Delhi, India.*

Right *A modern brick with a hollow, or "frog," in the top.*

4

There are often two types of holes in bricks, "frogs" or "cores." A frog is filled with mortar to make a stronger wall. A core hole makes the brick lighter.

Bricks are made at a brickworks.

Billions of bricks are used all over the world every year. The United States alone produces about 6.5 billion bricks a year. Bricks can be made of different **materials** and are used in many ways. This book looks at the many different kinds of bricks and how they are made and used.

Why use bricks?

We all need buildings as places where we can live and work in safety and comfort. Builders usually use whatever materials they can find locally for building. Stone and wood are often used, but they both have drawbacks. Stone buildings are very strong and last a long time, but stone is very heavy, expensive, and can be difficult to work with. Wood is cheaper and easier to use, but it needs to be taken care of to keep it from rotting or burning.

A wooden building such as this house in Utah is easily damaged by storms and floods.

Many parts of the world do not have large supplies of stone or wood, but most places have plenty of clay or mud that can be used to make bricks. Bricks are useful because they are fairly easy to make and use and are cheap to produce. They are also very strong, last a long time, and can look very attractive.

Above *Patterns in bricks can make walls look attractive.*

Below *Bricks are useful because they can be cut and split in many ways.*

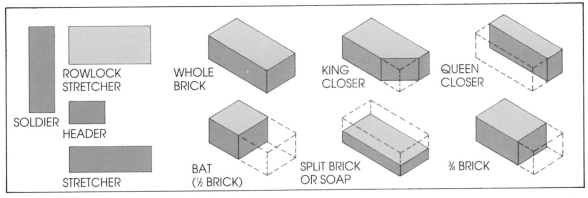

ROWLOCK STRETCHER

SOLDIER

HEADER

STRETCHER

WHOLE BRICK

BAT (½ BRICK)

KING CLOSER

SPLIT BRICK OR SOAP

QUEEN CLOSER

¾ BRICK

The history of bricks

Bricks are one of the world's oldest building materials. The first bricks were made in the Middle East about 10,000 years ago from the mud left behind after rivers had flooded. These bricks were molded by hand into the shape of small loaves of French bread. They were left to dry in the sun, then stuck together with mud or **tar** to make walls. The ancient city of Ur, in modern Iraq, was built with mud bricks in about 4000 B.C.

Brickmakers soon found that they could make stronger bricks by burning them in a fire. The art of making these strong bricks then began to spread east and west.

The art of making bricks spread west from the Middle East toward Egypt. This wall engraving shows how the ancient Egyptians made bricks.

The Great Fire of London destroyed the city's wooden buildings. They were replaced by stone and brick structures.

The Great Wall of China was built with bricks in 210 B.C., and the Romans used bricks throughout the great Roman Empire.

The Great Wall of China was built thousands of years ago. It is 1,500 miles long and is built of bricks.

Many of these brick buildings still stand today because they are strong and resistant to fire. A few hundred years ago, there were many terrible fires, such as the Great Fire of London in 1666, in European cities. The cities burned because they were built of wood. They were then rebuilt with bricks to make them more fireproof. Bricks became more and more popular, and were used to build the new homes and factories that were needed during the **Industrial Revolution**.

Mud bricks

Mud bricks are made from mud or clay and are simply left to dry in the sun. They are not as strong as bricks that have been fired in a kiln, but they are a very useful building material if they are kept dry.

In many countries, such as India and Malawi, the mud is pressed into **molds** by hand. It is sometimes mixed with straw, animal hair, or cow dung to make the bricks stronger. The bricks are then stuck together with liquid mud or clay to build walls.

Mud bricks are made by hand and are left to dry in the sun.

Arab builders use mud bricks to build thick walls with tiny windows. This keeps out the sun's heat. In Mexico, dried clay blocks are used to make **adobe** walls. Liquid clay is smeared on the outside for a smooth surface. The roofs of some adobe houses hang out over the walls to protect the walls from rain.

Adobe houses in New Mexico are built with mud bricks and are coated with liquid clay to give them a smooth finish.

11

Digging clay

At one time, all the clay needed for making bricks was dug out by hand, using spades to cut the clay into blocks. The clay was then taken to a brickworks by wheelbarrow or horse and cart. Clay is still dug by hand in some parts of the world, but it is very hard work because the clay is heavy, sticky, and hard to dig.

Modern brickworks use so much clay that huge machines, such as diggers, bulldozers, and scrapers, are used in large clay pits. Sometimes, a long chain of buckets, called a "dragline," digs the clay from as deep as 65 feet.

Big machines are used at clay pits for digging and moving clay.

The clay is then taken to the brickworks on a conveyor belt or in large dump trucks.

Restored clay pits have been made into lakes for leisure activities.

When a clay pit has been emptied of clay, it leaves a large, ugly hole in the countryside. But old clay pits have several uses. Sometimes they are filled with garbage then covered with soil and used for farming or growing trees. Clay pits can also be filled with water to make beautiful lakes.

Handmade bricks

All bricks used to be made by hand, and the art of making bricks by hand has not really changed for thousands of years.

First, the clay is crushed into small pieces and is mixed with water until it is soft. The brickmaker then cuts off a lump of clay, rolls it in sand, and pushes it firmly into a wooden mold, which has the "frog" at the bottom.

Making bricks by hand by using a wooden mold.

14

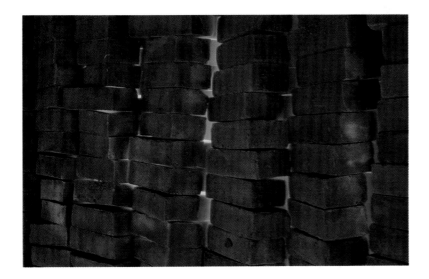

A stack of bricks is fired in a kiln to make the bricks harder and stronger.

If the brickmaker has used too much clay, he or she cuts it off by pulling a wire across the top of the mold. The brick is then tipped out of the mold and is stacked in a drying room. Soft bricks are called "green" bricks and take about a week to dry.

The bricks are then stacked in a kiln, which is like a large oven. They are fired for two or three days at over 2,000°F and are then left to cool. Even a skilled brickmaker only makes between 800 and 1,000 bricks a day. This means that handmade bricks are very expensive, but they are still used for special jobs such as restoring old buildings.

Machine-made bricks

The first machines that made bricks were driven by steam, and the bricks were fired by using wood or coal as fuel. Modern machinery is powered by electricity and gas to fire the kilns. Machine-made bricks are much quicker and cheaper to make than handmade bricks, and just a few people are needed to make many thousands of bricks a day.

This diagram shows how bricks are made by the process of extrusion.

There are several ways of making bricks by machine, but the most popular is by **extrusion** and wire cutting.

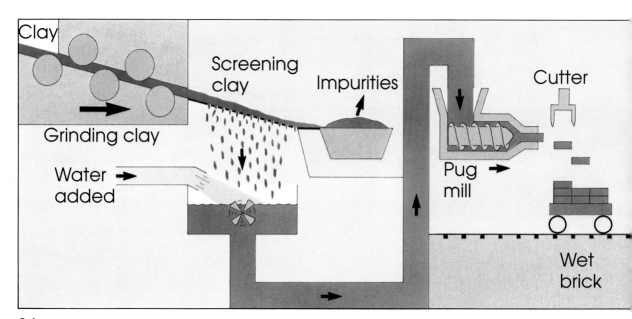

Clay

Grinding clay

Water added

Screening clay

Impurities

Cutter

Pug mill

Wet brick

To do this, the clay is ground and mixed and then forced, or extruded, through a machine. This makes a long, square-shaped bar of stiff clay, which is then cut to exactly the right size by wire cutters.

The bricks are carried to the drying rooms, where they are placed in large racks for a few days. Then the bricks are put on trucks that are pushed slowly through a tunnel kiln. Here the bricks are fired and cooled. A modern kiln can take as many as 80,000 bricks at a time. The whole brick-making process only takes about eleven days.

Above *Dried "green" bricks are stacked in a kiln, ready for firing.*

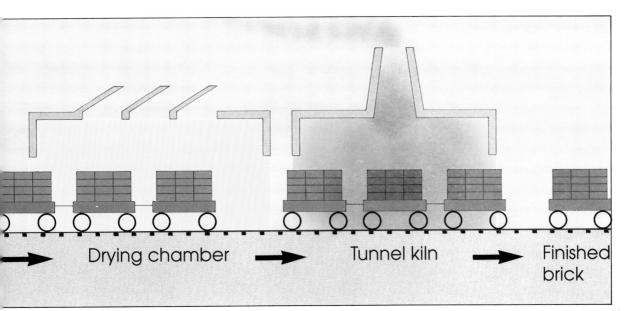

Drying chamber ➔ Tunnel kiln ➔ Finished brick

Transporting bricks

Stacks of bricks in a builder's yard, ready to be moved to a building site.

Large quantities of bricks are very heavy and difficult to transport. In the past, there were many small brickworks, each one built near the town where the bricks were used. The only way of moving the bricks from the brickworks to the building site was by horse-drawn cart. In the eighteenth and nineteenth centuries, canal barges were often used for transporting bricks over longer distances. Later, trains and steam-powered trucks were used to do this, but the bricks still had to be loaded and unloaded by hand.

Large quantities of bricks can be moved quickly and easily with a forklift.

18

In a modern brickworks, the bricks are packed in cubes of about 500, wrapped in plastic, and strapped together with metal bands. All this is done by machine, saving a lot of time, effort, and money. The bricks are then taken to the building site on a special truck. The truck has its own small crane on the back for lifting the packages of bricks on and off the truck.

A mobile crane is used to lift a stack of concrete blocks.

Building with bricks

Although bricks are now made and transported by machines, they still have to be laid by hand. Bricklaying is very skilled work. A bricklayer builds a wall by placing the bricks on top of each other in layers called **courses**. Using a pointed **trowel**, the bricklayer covers each course of bricks with a layer of mortar. This is a mixture of **cement**, sand, and water. The mortar sticks the bricks together, and sets very hard when it is dry.

A bricklayer lays bricks in courses that are held together by mortar.

BRICK BONDS

COMMON (HEADER) bond has a series of headers (short sides) breaking each sixth row.

RUNNING (or STRETCHER) bond, the most common, is laid in overlapping courses of stretchers (bricks' long sides).

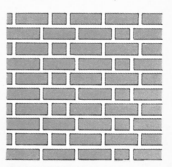

GARDEN WALL, a strong bond, has a symmetrical placing of the headers in every other course.

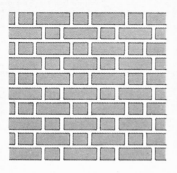

FLEMISH bond has the headers and stretchers alternately laid in every course.

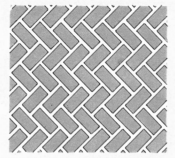

HERRINGBONE bond, used in paving or paneling, may be laid with the brick flat or on edge.

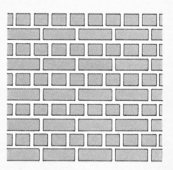

ENGLISH bond has the vertical mortar joint one third from the end of each stretcher brick.

Bricklayers also use a **plumb line** and a **spirit level** to make sure that the brickwork is straight and level. The bricks are laid in patterns, called **bonds**, to make sure that the vertical joints between each brick do not meet. If the bricks were simply stacked on top of each other in straight lines, the wall would be very weak and might soon collapse.

A diagram showing the different patterns, or bonds, that can be made with bricks.

Special bricks

Bricks come in many different sizes, shapes, and colors, and they all have their own special uses. Firebricks, for example, are made from a special clay and do not crack under intense heat. They are used to line fireplaces, kilns, and furnaces.

These special bricks are used for making pavement in Saudi Arabia.

Engineering bricks are strong and hard. They are used to build walls that support the weight of heavy structures like bridges.

Glass bricks are often used inside buildings to let in light.

Pavements and floors are made with bricks called "pavers." Stable pavers are bricks with grooves that provide extra grip for people to walk on and drainage to take away water from the pavement's surface.

Not all bricks are made of clay. Some modern bricks are made of concrete, and others are made of sand and **lime**. Walls can also be made of glass bricks. This lets plenty of light into a building. Glass bricks are made in several different colors and are often used in office buildings.

Making concrete blocks

These concrete blocks have been made by hand. Liquid concrete is poured into molds and is allowed to set.

Concrete is a mixture of cement, water, and stones. It dries out and sets to form a very hard building material. Concrete was first used by the Romans, and it is still widely used in the modern building industry. To make concrete blocks, liquid concrete is poured into molds and the concrete is then allowed to set.

Builders laying courses of concrete blocks. It is quick and easy to build with concrete blocks.

Concrete blocks are much larger than bricks. They are also cheaper because they do not need to be fired. They are not as strong as bricks, but they are much easier and quicker to work with.

Many modern walls have bricks on the outside and concrete blocks on the inside.

Modern buildings often have walls in which the outer part of the wall is made of bricks and the inner part is made of concrete blocks. Between the two is an air gap, which helps to keep the building warm in winter and cool in summer. Modern lightweight concrete blocks can also be made by bubbling air through the concrete before it sets. These blocks provide good **insulation**.

Making soil bricks

In developing countries, concrete and bricks are often expensive. Until recently, some people in these countries had to rely on hand-molded mud bricks to build new homes, schools, and factories. Mud bricks, however, are not very strong, and they are easily damaged by heavy rain.

A recent invention now allows people to make bricks quickly and cheaply. The invention is a simple hand-pressing machine, which uses a mixture of soil, water,

This recently invented block-making machine makes cheap bricks from a mixture of soil, water, and cement.

and a small amount of cement (or lime). It is easy to use and produces strong soil blocks that can be used in the same way as bricks. By using this machine, six people can produce sixty blocks an hour. Buildings made from these blocks can last for up to thirty years.

These new houses in a village in Kenya were built with soil bricks.

This method has already been used to build new villages in Kenya, Nigeria, and the Caribbean, and will soon be helping to build new homes in many other parts of the world.

Projects with bricks

Make your own bricks

You will need:

Modeling clay in two colors
Matchboxes

A craft knife
A rolling pin

1. Push lumps of modeling clay of one color firmly into the trays from the matchboxes to shape them. Then empty your modeling clay shapes onto a table.

2. Using a craft knife (with an adult's help), cut each piece of modeling clay across its width into three equal pieces. These are your bricks.

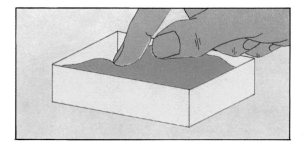

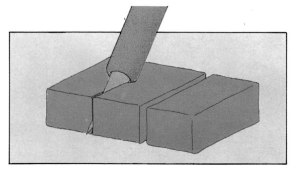

3. Using the other color of modeling clay, roll out a thin sheet, and cut it into small pieces to fit between your bricks. This will be your mortar.

4. Use your modeling clay bricks and mortar to build a wall.

Try making the main patterns, or bonds, with your bricks. Turn to page 21 and try to follow the example of each bond shown.

Make a clay pot

You will need:

Pottery clay
A craft knife

A rolling pin
Water

1. Knead the clay until it is soft, and roll it out on a flat surface by using a rolling pin.

2. When the clay is about ½ inch thick, with an adult's help cut out the base of your pot.

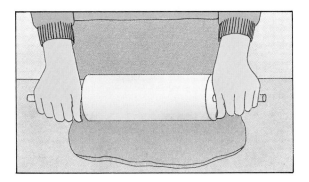

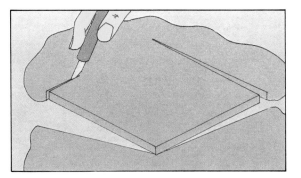

3. Cut out two sides the same length as the base and stick onto the base by using a little water.

4. Cut out two more pieces of clay to fit at the ends of your pot. Seal all the edges with water.

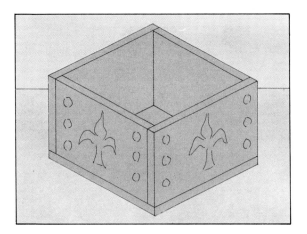

5. Cover your pot, and let it stand for several days in a warm, airy place to dry.

If your school has a kiln, ask your teacher to fire your pot to make it stronger and longer-lasting.

Glossary

Adobe Adobe walls are made of clay bricks that are left to dry in the sun.

Bond The pattern of bricks in a wall. The bricks are arranged to overlap to give the wall strength.

Cement A fine, powdery material that sets hard when mixed with water.

Courses Even, horizontal layers of bricks in a wall.

Extrusion When a material is squeezed out of a machine to produce a particular shape.

Industrial Revolution The period during the eighteenth and nineteenth centuries when industry and mechanization began to develop and expand.

Insulation The prevention of heat loss or gain in a building.

Kiln A large oven used for firing bricks, pottery, or glass.

Lime A chemical found in certain rocks. It was originally used to make mortar before the invention of cement.

Material A substance that can be used to make something.

Mortar A mixture of cement, sand, and water that is used to stick stones and bricks together.

Mold A container that is used to give something a shape.

Plumb line A piece of string with a weight on the lower end. It is used to check that something is vertical.

Spirit level A tool used to check that a surface is level. It is usually a length of wood or metal, with an air bubble inside a sealed tube of fluid. When the bubble is in the middle of the tube, the surface is level.

Tar A black, sticky substance formed from coal, wood, or peat.

Trowel A flat, pointed, triangular hand tool used by bricklayers to spread mortar.

Books to read

Bates, Robert L. *Stone, Clay, Glass: How Building Materials Are Found and Used*. Hillside, NJ: Enslow, 1987.

Cash, Terry. *Bricks*. Ada, Okla.: Garrett Educational Corp., 1990.

Hamilton-MacLaren, Alistair. *Houses and Homes*. Technology Projects. New York: Bookwright, 1992.

Lambert, Christopher. *Building Technology*. Technology in Action. New York: Bookwright, 1991.

Whyman, Kathryn. *Structures and Materials*. Science Today. New York: Gloucester, 1987.

Useful addresses

Brick Institute of America
11490 Commerce Park Drive
Reston, VA 22091-1525

National Association of
Brick Distributors
1600 Spring Hill Road
Vienna, VA 22180

Acknowledgments

Thomson Learning would like to thank Brian E. Trimble and the Brick Institute of America for reviewing the original text and providing additional information to include in the book.

Index

Picture acknowledgments

The publishers would like to thank the following for allowing their photographs to be reproduced in this book: Building Research Establishment (David Webb), 26, 27; Cephas Picture Library (Mick Rock), 6, 14, 17, 18 (bottom); Chapel Studios (Zul Mukhida), *cover* (bottom), 7, 15, 20, 25 (bottom); C. M. Dixon, *cover* (top); Mary Evans, 8, 9, (top); Eye Ubiquitous (Paul Seheult), 4 (bottom), 19, 25 (top); the Hutchison Library, *title page*, 10 (Chris Parker), 22 (Bernard Gerard); J. Allen Cash Ltd, 13; Panos Pictures, 5 (Neil Cooper), 24 (Marc French); Photri, 9 (bottom), 23; Graham Rickard, 18 (top); Sefton Photo Library, 12; Wayland Picture Library (Jimmy Holmes), 4 (top); Zefa Picture Library, 11. All artwork is by Jenny Hughes.